SOUTH AFRICA

SOUTH AFRICA

Jean Morris

PURNELL

Cape Town · Johannesburg · London

Published by Purnell & Sons (S.A.) (Pty) Ltd.
70 Keerom Street, Cape Town, South Africa.

© Jean Morris 1971

Library of Congress Catalog Card No. 74-170360

SBN 360 00143 2

Design and artwork by Jean Morris.

Set in 6 on 7 pt and 9 on 10 pt Univers Medium Expanded.

Lithographic Positives by Hirt & Carter (Pty) Ltd., Cape Town.
(From 35 mm. transparencies.)

Printed in the Republic of South Africa by
Associated Printing & Publishing Co. (Pty) Ltd., Cape Town.

Bound in South Africa by E. Seabrook, Cape Town.

In 1647 a ship of the Dutch East India Company was wrecked in Table Bay. The survivors managed to get most of the cargo ashore and lived in the then unknown land until 1648 when a fleet of company ships returning from the East put in for water and took the survivors back to Holland. These men sang the praises of the great bay below a table-top mountain, and the captain presented a report to the directors of the Company, suggesting that a victualling station be established there. The Cape of Good Hope was a natural half-way house between Holland and the East and it was a welcome stop for the weary mariners, for conditions were so appalling on the old sailing ships that many did not even survive the three month voyage to the Cape.

And so it was that in 1652 the first white settlement in South Africa was established on the shores of Table Bay. The first settlers endured great hardships in colonising this land which until then had been inhabited only by the nomadic Bushmen and Hottentot tribes. Their principal settlement around Table Bay was eventually to become the city of Cape Town, which is today the legislative capital and one of the most important seaports on the continent of Africa.

For more than three hundred years this city and the peninsula on which it was built have cast their spell over all who have visited them. Sir Francis Drake described it as "the fairest Cape in the circumference of the earth". Part of the charm of Cape Town lies in the fact that it was once a place where East met West. The Dutch brought to the Cape slaves from the East Indies, and Malay craftsmen, and the descendants of these Malays, a proud and skilled community, have always kept themselves apart from the other sections of the population. You can still see fezzed men answering the call to prayer from the muezzin in the mosques not far from the centre of Cape Town.

The Dutch originated the Cape style of architecture, cool gabled houses with white-washed walls, thatched roofs, large high-ceilinged rooms, shuttered to keep out the heat of summer. They also laid out the broad streets of the old towns and planted the beautiful oaks which we still see today. The renowned wines and brandies of the Cape owe their existence to the French Huguenot settlers, who brought with them their traditional wine-making skills.

In 1812 the British took over the Cape from the Dutch and established it as a colony. They encouraged a wider settlement of the Cape, and in 1820 arranged for settlers from Britain to colonise the Eastern Cape to counter the marauding African tribes who had by this time reached this area, having gradually moved down the eastern coast from Central and East Africa. The Dutch became dissatisfied with the British rule and moved into the interior, travelling the rough country in ox-wagons, establishing their own settlements and farms and ultimately their own republic.

No visitor to South Africa should ever leave the country without touring the Cape Peninsula on one of the magnificent roads that pass through mountainous coastal scenery, above the bays and beaches that are some of the most famous South African seaside resorts. Within a range of a hundred miles of Cape Town are magnificent historic farmhouses and vineyards to be visited and wines to be tasted. There are mountains to be climbed, well-stocked trout streams that can be fished, and many excellent golf courses near to Cape Town itself.

Far to the north-west of Cape Town is the virtually uninhabited region of Namaqualand where, following the spring rains, the generally barren land becomes carpeted with indigenous wild flowers of every colour. Everyone who has seen the wild flowers of Namaqualand will agree that they are one of the most beautiful sights, and botanists from all over the world have come to see them. In the Cape Peninsula alone there are more than 2 600 different species of wild flowers.

There are three main routes out of Cape Town, the principal road to the Transvaal cities of Johannesburg and Pretoria, the eastern coastal road incorporating the "Garden Route", and the road to South West Africa, via Namaqualand. The road to Johannesburg, over Du Toit's Kloof mountain pass, climbs up through the Hex River mountains, after which it runs straight for hundreds of kilometres through the arid Karoo, where some seven or eight million sheep flourish on farms, many of which are larger than fifty thousand hectares. This gives a first glimpse of what are truly the wide open spaces of South Africa. This main road then leads on to the city of Kimberley, the centre of the uncut diamond trade. Diamonds to the value of R130 000 000 per year are handled by the offices of the diamond companies. The road climbs gradually upward to an altitude of 1 700 m above sea level to Johannesburg the biggest mining city in the world, and to Pretoria, administrative capital of the Republic. You can drive the 1 570 km from Cape Town to Johannesburg in two days, fly in less than two hours, or make the same journey by train in a day and a half. It took the early pioneers travelling by ox-wagon six months to do the journey.

The eastern route out of Cape Town follows the coast, passing through Mossel Bay, George, Knysna, Port Elizabeth, East London and Durban, and is known as the "Garden Route", and the wise traveller will allow several days for this tour. To the north of George over the Outeniqua Mountains lies the town of Oudtshoorn, famous for its ostrich farms and near to the Cango Caves. The coastal road passes through the Wilderness, Knysna, Plettenberg Bay, and other little hamlets on the coast where many families have holiday houses. A mile or two inland from these resorts lies the immense Tzitzikama Forest, once inhabited by vast herds of elephant. This is one of the most interesting primeval forests in the world where some of the trees are well over a thousand years old and have grown to a height of 50 m or more. It was the indigenous timber that brought the first settlers to Knysna. They needed the wood for building ships, jetties, wagons and for floors and rafters in their houses. Van Plettenberg, one of the governors of the Cape during the rule of the Dutch East India Company, explored this area in the 18th Century and decided that its bays and rivers surpassed even the natural beauties found near Cape Town.

The road then leads to the lovely coastal cities and holiday resorts of Port Elizabeth, the centre of the motor industry, and East London. Then inland through the Transkei, now one of the independent Bantu states and home of the Xhosa people, who are one of the largest Bantu tribes in South Africa, numbering over four million. They live very much as they have always lived, in grass huts surrounded by the maize fields that supply their staple diet. The civil administration of the Transkei was transferred to the Xhosa people in 1963 and there are now some two thousand Bantu civil servants at work. Umtata is now the capital of this Bantu "homeland". Beyond it the vegetation changes and gradually gives way to sub-tropical banana plantations and, further on, huge fields of sugar cane. This is Natal, the "Garden Province" of the Republic.

Natal became a British colony in 1842 after Britain had annexed the harbour and the coast surrounding it. The magnificent land-locked bay, entered by a narrow channel, was originally called Port Natal because the Portuguese had discovered it on Christmas Day. The British renamed the harbour after the Governor of the Cape Colony, Sir Benjamin D'Urban.

Natal is the smallest of the four provinces of South Africa, the provincial capital being the beautiful inland town of Pietermaritzburg. Bustling Durban is now the third biggest city in South Africa and as a port is second largest on all the coasts of Africa. Through Durban flows the bulk of all the merchandise imported by the Transvaal, including technical equipment and stores required by the mines of the Witwatersrand and the Orange Free State goldfields. It is also the centre of the sugar industry. Along one hundred and sixty kilometres of the coastal belt of Natal there are sugar plantations and mills producing two million tons of sugar a year for the home market and for export.

The other great Natal industry is tourism. In the winter this stretch of the South African coast has an almost perfect climate and in that season of the year, from May to August, Durban's excellent hotels and the seaside resorts south and north of the city are packed with holiday-makers. Natal's population temporarily increases by about 250 000 during the winter season. The people of Natal know how to cater for visitors. The hotels have large staffs and excellent service. The food is first-class, with oysters available, fresh lobsters, prawns and tasty fish of many varieties. Add to the menu exotic fruits such as paw-paws, avocado pears, mangoes and pineapples, and you have meals fit for the gourmets of the world. In winter, horse racing is the ruling passion of all Natalians, and the South African classic, the Durban July Handicap, is run on the Durban Turf Club's renowned Greyville Course, which is close to the centre of the town.

North-west of Durban lies Zululand, home of the Zulu people, who number over four million, or more than the total European population of South Africa. The Zulus can still be seen following their original way of life, and the patterns in the beadwork of their adornments still convey a form of language between them. Every year there is the religious Shembi festival, and they come for hundreds of kilometres to gather in memory of Chaka Zulu, their revered Chief. This ceremony lasts for a week and culminates in four days of non-stop dancing. Both the Hluhluwe Game Reserve and the Umfolozi Reserve, famous for the square-lipped white rhinoceros, are located in Zululand.

The Drakensberg Mountains, a magnificent range of peaks, some of which are over 3 300 m high, are adequately served by National Parks and many fine hotels, and provide activities such as walking, mountain climbing, riding, trout fishing, tennis and bowls, in the crisp champagne air.

To the west of Natal stretches the Orange Free State, with Bloemfontein, "Fountain of Flowers", judicial capital of the Republic. The Orange Free State is the fifth largest maize producer in the world, and is a country of flat rolling plains.

Durban and Johannesburg are connected by 720 km of excellent road, or a night's journey by rail. There are also excellent air services, the flight takes just under an hour and is so popular that there are as many as 10 flights a day in the holiday season.

Johannesburg, in the Transvaal, by far the biggest city in South Africa, is not yet one hundred years old. It is not only the largest mining city in the world but also one of the most unusual. It was first established as a mining camp on a barren, rocky triangle of ground. It had no great expectation of life, for gold mines did not last very long in those days. However, these mines proved to be the exception. Some of the old mines on which the prosperity of Johannesburg and South Africa was founded, have only just come to the end of their lives, having produced gold for eighty years or longer. Without the gold and the diamond mines, South Africa would not have developed its manufacturing industries as rapidly as it has done. In addition to gold and diamonds,

South Africa has a fantastic wealth of other minerals, some of great strategic importance, such as uranium which is a by-product of the gold mines. Added to these riches, are the world's largest known reserves of chromite, immense coal fields, large deposits of iron ore and platinum.

From the air, as you begin the descent to Jan Smuts airport, Johannesburg looks very much like any other sprawling industrial city, until you notice the great mine dumps — the bigger the dump the older and deeper the mine. Most of the ground south and east of Johannesburg is undermined to a depth of between 2 000 and 3 000 m. Below the surface there are hundreds of kilometres of passages, hewn from solid rock, where thousands of mine workers have toiled for years to produce gold. The gold mining industry of South Africa has produced ore to the value of almost R18 000 000 000, representing 76% of the free world's supply.

Johannesburg itself is a city of tall buildings, utilitarian rather than beautiful, bustling with activity and inhabited by more than a million people, of whom slightly less than half are White, the others being Bantu, Coloured and Asians.

Whatever the city itself lacks in beauty is more than made up for by the beautiful gardens of its prosperous residential suburbs. Johannesburg has one of the most agreeable climates anywhere in the world — no rain whatever in the winter months, but sparkling sunshine nine hours a day to offset the cold. The moment the first showers fall, usually in September, the country turns from sunbaked brown to brilliant green.

In the surrounding rocky terrain of Johannesburg there are virtually no natural amenities. The result has been that the people of Johannesburg have always had to contrive their own amusements. They have more swimming pools than any other city of comparable size in the world. They also have about 40 golf courses and a vast number of tennis courts. The city also has many theatres which present a wide variety of entertainment.

Thirty five miles north of Johannesburg is Pretoria, the administrative capital of South Africa. It would be difficult to find two cities in one province of a country so near in distance and yet so different. Pretoria has less than half the population and is quieter and more relaxed than Johannesburg. It is a city built on a plain, encircled by hills. On one of these hills stand the massive Union Buildings, which contain the offices of the Prime Minister and his Cabinet Ministers and of senior civil servants. Here all major decisions of policy are taken, and later presented to Parliament when it meets in Cape Town to debate the measures proposed by the Government.
Pretoria at most seasons of the year is a beautiful city, especially so in the spring

when the jacaranda trees that line every street produce a mass of light purple blooms which carpet the ground with shades of mauve when falling.

Twenty five kilometres beyond Pretoria lives the Ndebele tribe, renowned for the brightly coloured patterns painted on the outside walls of their houses. This painting is always done by the womenfolk, who also spend many hours on intricate bead handcraft.

The two cities of Johannesburg and Pretoria stand on the great central plateau that in the Transvaal is called the "Highveld". 320 km beyond Pretoria, on the road that leads to the north-east, the descent from this plateau begins. Three hours after leaving the brisk cool air of the Highveld you have dropped some 1 300 m, almost to sea level, and you are then in the warm, sub-tropical sunshine. The Highveld of the Transvaal, and the Lowveld which you reach after this somewhat abrupt descent, are like two different countries, with different weather conditions, different geological formations, and different Bantu tribes as their inhabitants.

Not far below the escarpment is the world-famous Kruger National Park where the wild animals of Africa live exactly as they lived before human beings inhabited the country. This wildlife sanctuary is visited by 370 000 people a year and is the largest of the ten National Game Parks in South Africa.

The impression persists among people who have never toured in the Transvaal that it is largely a barren waste, parts of which are green to look upon only after the summer rains have fallen. This is quite untrue. The escarpment of the Drakensberg range, where it descends to the Lowveld, is as wildly beautiful as anything in Africa. The foothills of the Drakensberg and the massive granite buttresses of the escarpment in the area add grandeur to the scene. Here are the rivers and streams that are missing on the Highveld, and dense vegetation is nourished by a consistent rainfall.

In the past the difficulty lay in getting to these places. There were few roads and even the ox wagons could not fight their way up and down many of the precipitous slopes. Today there are magnificent roads and every amenity for travellers. This area of the Transvaal has become a holiday-maker's paradise, where tourists pause and relax on their journeys to and from the Kruger National Park.

This photographic book shows some of the facets of this beautiful country and its people. The population of over twenty-one million consists of nearly four million Whites, fifteen million Bantu, two million Coloureds and over half a million Asians. This is a land of great wealth and vitality where cities, crammed with sky-scrapers and every modern amenity, contrast with the rich heritage of natural beauty.

CONTENTS

CAPE   Plates: 1–74

Cape Peninsula
Cape Town
Wine districts
Western Cape
Garden Route
Transkei

NATAL   Plates: 75–122

Durban
Zululand
Hluhluwe
Drakensberg Mountains

ORANGE FREE STATE   Plates: 123–125

Bloemfontein

TRANSVAAL   Plates: 126–153

Johannesburg
Mine dancers
Pretoria
Ndebele Tribe
Kruger National Park

Cape Town Harbour

2. Early morning, Cape Town Dock

3. Table Mountain from Melkbosstrand

4. Spring Flowers, Table Mountain

5. Cape Town from Signal Hill

6. View of Sea Point from Signal Hil

7. Overlooking Lion's Head from the top of Table Mountain

8. Camps Bay from Kloof Road

Oudekraal, with view of Lion's Head

10. Sand dunes, Hout Bay

1. Cape Coloured girl, Hout Bay

12. Fishing Boats at Hout Bay harbour

13. Mending the fishing nets, Hout Bay

4, A patchwork of fishing nets at Hout Bay harbour

15.   Snoek boats – Hout Ba

6. Kronendal, Cape Dutch homestead, Hout Bay

17. Chapman's Peak Drive, Cape Peninsula

3. Noordhoek

19. Cape of Good Hope

20. Bontebok

21. Baboon, Cape Peninsula

22. Towards Chapmans Peak

23. Flamingos near Strandfontein

24. Muizenberg from Strandfontein Beach

25.   Zeekoevlei Yacht Club, Cape

6. Clifton, Cape

27. Cliftor

8. Clifton Beach

29. Sunset at Clifton

31. Sea Point beachfront, Cape Town

2. The Nico Malan Opera House, Cape Town

33. Cape Town, New Statio

4.　Malay flower seller

35. The Old Fishing Harbour, Cape Town

36. Malay flower seller

37. The Trust Bank Centre, Cape Town

48. The Houses of Parliament, Cape Town

39. Malay Mosque, Cape Town

40. The Malay game of Kerrim

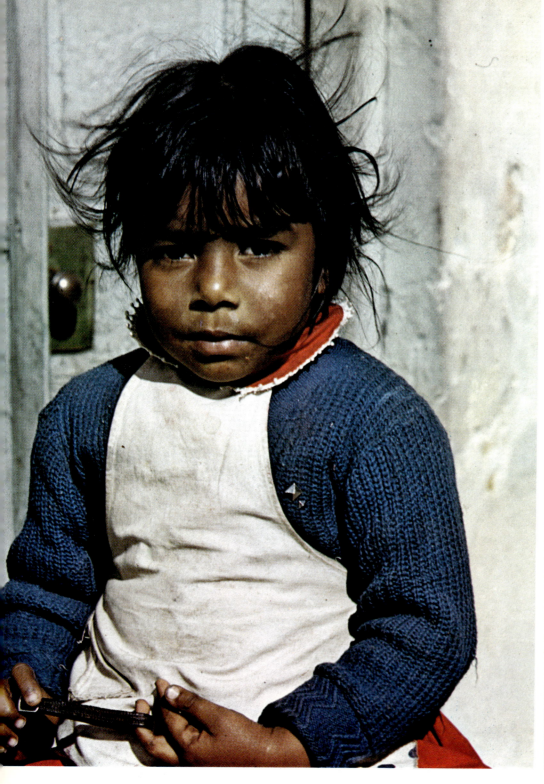

41. Cape Malay children

42. Cape Malay child

43.   Cape Coloured coons at the Annual Coon Carniva

14. Coons

45. Groot Constanti

3. The wine cellars at Groot Constantia

47.   Autumn Vineyards, Cape

8. Lanzerac, Stellenbosch, Cape

49.   The old slave bell, Lanzer

). Die Burgerhuis, Stellenbosch

51. Coloured farm workers' cottages at Banhoek

62. Coloured farm-hand and child

53. Protea, South Africa's national flower

54. Forestry Reserve, Franschhoek, Cape

55. Banhoek, Cape

56. Franschhoek Valley, Cape

57. Aloes

58. Winter Orchard, Franschhoek

59. Du Toit's Kloof, Cape

30. Elands River, beyond du Toit's Kloof, Cape

61. Winter sunshine Cape

82. Winter in the Hex River Valley, Cape

63. Langebaan, Cap

64. Cape Spring flowers

65.   Wheat fields of the Western Cape

6. Wheat fields, Cape

67.   The Outeniqua Pas

8. The Wilderness, Cape

69.   Stormy sea at Knysna Heads, Cape

70. Ostrich at an ostrich farm, Oudtshoorn, Cape

71. The Transkei

72. Xhosa women of the Transkei

73. Prickly pear

74. Xhosa herdsmen

75. Natal North Coast Beach

76. Durban

77. Zulu Ricksha Boys

78. African native market, Durban

79. The Old Indian Market, Durban

81. Zulu Chief

82. Zulu War Dance

3. Zulu dancers

84. Wild banana palm, Durban South Coast

85. Cutting sugar car

6.   Cane fields

87. Cut canefield

38. Pondo woman carrying firewood

89. Yellow Poinsettia
90. Bougainvillae

91. Kaffirboom

92.   African native market, south coast, Natal

93. Selling avocado pears

94. African native pottery

95.   Weaving mats

96. Zulu war dancers, at the annual religious Shembi Festival on the north coast of Natal

97. Zulu maidens

98. Zulu matrons

39. Zulu woman, her hair plaited with string and mud

100. Zulu spectators

01. At the bus stop, Mtubatuba, Zululand

102. Shoppers, Mtubatuba African marke

03. Zulu girl, her hair plaited with dry grass

104. Pondo girl

105. Hluhluwe Game Reserve, Zululand

06. Square-lipped white rhino, Hluhluwe Game Reserve

107.   Impala, Hluhluwe

08. Impala

109.   Valley of a Thousand Hills, Natal

10. Zulu girl, Pietermaritzburg native market

111. Indian girl, Pietermaritzburg native market

112. The Berg River at Underberg, Nata

113. Fishing cottage at Underberg

114.   Native trading station at the foot of Sani Pass leading into Lesotho

115. Drakensberg Gardens, Natal

116. Drakensberg Gardens, Natal

17. Basuto native hut

118. Basuto native girl

119. Cathedral Peak in the Drakensberg Mountains, Nata

20. Bushmen rock paintings, Drakensberg Mountains

121. Early morning, National Park, Drakensberg Mountains

22. National Park in the Drakensberg Mountains

123.   Africaner cattle, Orange Free State

24. Countryside, Orange Free State

125. Bloemfontein, capital of the Orange Free State, from Naval Hill

26.   Waterskiing early morning on the Vaal River, Transvaal

127. Wild cosmos lining the road to Johannesburg

128. Selling naartjies, outside Johannesburg, Transvaal

129.   Johannesburg seen from the top of the new Standard Bank building

130. The Standard Bank Centre, Johannesburg

131. Penny Whistle "Kwela" music – Johannesburg

132. Mine band at the Johannesburg mine dancing — xylophone players

133.   Sunday morning tribal dancing at a Johannesburg gold mine

134. Mine dancers

135. Xhosa tribal dancers

136. Mine dancers

37.   Union Buildings, Pretoria, Transvaal

138. Basket seller, Ndebele village, Transvaal

39.   Ndebele woman

140.   Walls of the Ndebele village houses, painted by the women fol

141. Bead necklaces and beaded belts, made by the Ndebele women

142. Ndebele child and baby

143. Polishing the brass leg bracelets

144. Ndebele beadcraft

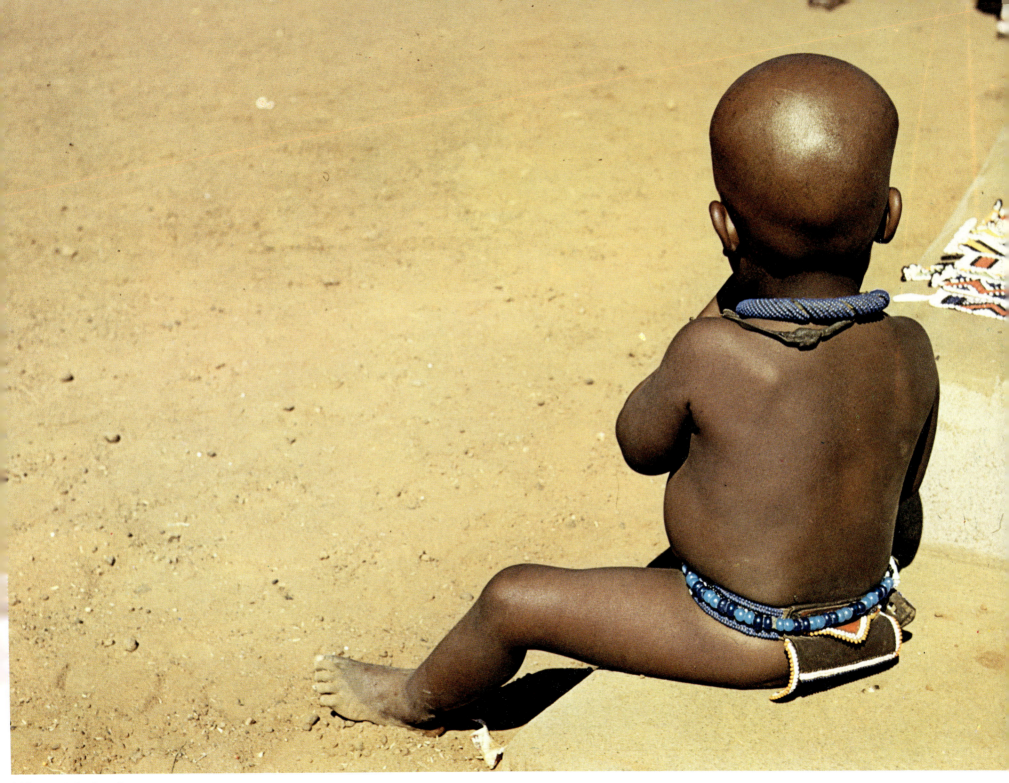

145. Ndebele piccanin

146.   The Kruger Park, Transvaal — elephants

147. Lions

148. Giraffe

49. Zebra

150. Weaver birds' nests

51. Female kudu

53. Impala